IN DEFENSE OF DEFENSIVENESS

Knowing Our Defenses

Lowering Our Defenses

Living With Our Defenses

IN DEFENSE OF DEFENSIVENESS

Knowing Our Defenses
Lowering Our Defenses
Living With Our Defenses

K.L. Fischer PhD

K.L. Fischer Publications

Publisher: K.L. Fischer Publications

ISBN-13: 978-1539622598
ISBN-10: 1539622592

Table of Contents

Introduction

I suppose knowing a little about something is better than knowing a lot about nothing. But then, how do we reconcile this with – A little knowledge is a dangerous thing? Everyone seems to think they know something about, and have opinions about – politics, and religion . . . and let's add psychology to the mix.

We who are in the field have come to expect, what we have dubbed, "Armchair psychologizing." Well, let's see now, what are the more popular members of the "izing group?" There's politicizing, theologizing, philosophizing, and psychologizing. I think it's fair to say the one most people think they know the most about is Psychologizing – without question.

It's not a stretch to say that when the subject of psychology comes up (or any subject that is even remotely akin to it – which could be just about anything that has to do with people living their lives), lay people can't help but chime in with their thoughts and opinions. Armchair psychologizing is addictive, that's for sure. They all want to put in their two cents worth. That's OK. I completely understand the temptation and the inclination. In a way this may (in and of itself) be a testimony to the subject's relevancy – That we all have the confidence to take a crack at it.

I'm not one of those guys in my field who thinks he has all the answers. When some of my colleagues got their PhD – That's when pomposity set in. I give credit to my being forty-three at the time (and already by that time having been humbled by two other professions) that I skipped over the part of knowing it all.

Besides, the way I saw it was if just about everyone has something to say about something – That something must have some relevancy for them. Which validates for me that what I have to say has some relevancy for them. Which is all I can ask for at this time.

Psychological jargon as a function of armchair psychologizing is common parlance. Psychological terms have become part of everyday discourse. If there once was an ivory-tower-possessive-mentality –

that certain terms were indigenous to textbooks only – to be used only by those who truly understood their theoretical orientation – That time (I can only, truthfully, speak for myself) is long past.

In examining my own mind regarding what changes have occurred in my thinking from the time I was professor – classroom taught – (then began teaching what I was taught) . . . [I should stop my retro-thinking right here and remind myself, as I point out to you . . . That I never taught what I was taught – not literally] – I put my knowledge and my experience together with what I learned from profs and books. What came out was uniquely subjective, but at the same time, objectively relevant.

If there's one thread of common purpose that winds its way through the process of my teaching, psychotherapy and writing, it is Relevancy. The purpose of the process of sharing with you what comes from my mind and heart is that you are reached by the relevancy of my words to you – for you.

In the sense that relevancy can't be forced – It is not under my control – It happens – Or, it doesn't happen. I am dependent on you to expose yourselves to what I present. How you perceive my presentation – What you do with it – Whether it will be life changing for you, albeit, even in a small way . . . All of this has to do with whether or not you find it **relevant for you and yours**. I pray that you do – But if you don't – You don't. Try revisiting my book another day. Sometimes it's all about timing.

Moving away then from prof-taught, textbook theory which has generated a pedantic, didactic presentation and theoretically-bound compilation of psychological terms – I choose to present for your consideration a version and variation of my professional and perceptual understanding, conceptualization, and realistic life-grounded application of one such relevant psychological term. In plainer English, I intend to share with you what I have to say about a psychological term that has become part and parcel of everyday parlance – Defensiveness.

Keep in mind that I write from the perspective of a reality theorist and therapist. This means that I emphasize awareness of – and consciousness of – choices – We make – We own – We take responsibility for.

I talk about our personality evolving and expanding through person perception and self-experience. Our self-concept is formed from the perceptions we have of others' perceptions of us – our perceptions of others – our perceptions of ourselves. We make perceptual judgments based on the four aspects of person perception – Appearance; Mannerisms; How we say; What we say. Behavioral changes occur when we become aware of (insight) what we need to change in our presentation and are able to present, accordingly, in a different way.

In sum, then, this is the backdrop against which I want to share with you my **Fischerized** – conceptualized, reality-based application of **Defense Mechanisms** (The textbook term). **Defensiveness** is my colloquial term of choice.

Fischerized Defensiveness

The textbook rendition (With Freudian (Fr) Psychoanalytic (PAT) overtones) goes something like this . . . Defense Mechanisms (DMs) refer to "unconscious processes of the ego which keep disturbing and unacceptable impulses from being expressed directly."

I have no one-sentence definition to offer as a point of comparison or contrast. Even if I would be able to confine my conceptualizing to one sentence, I wouldn't try. What I have to say about DMs and **Defensiveness** in general, is so radically (in the best sense of the word) different and (from my perspective) so much closer to describing what **Defensiveness** is – i.e. How it works – What purpose it serves – There is enough to say to fill this book. [Moreover, it would be a waste of your time and mine for me to pick apart the textbook rendition – which for me (and I believe for you) has so little realistic relevancy.]

Defensiveness is inextricably connected with my theory of how our personality evolves and expands through person perception and self-experience. Our self-concept (i.e. the picture we have of ourselves) is formed (painted) using the brushes of person perception, i.e. our perception of others – of others' perception of us – of ourselves. A percept involves an interaction between a presenter and receiver. Perceptual judgments are made by both parties heavily influenced by what each participant brings to the situation of their respective personalities.

Our personalities are distinguished by the needs we have. We are perceived (and perceive ourselves) as having in common with others our survival needs. [I include the need for closeness in this group.] Our other-than-survival-needs may differ in kind as well as degree. Our personality needs are the motivators behind what and how and how much of our personality we present – Whether as a presenter – Proacting – Or a perceiver – Reacting.

That which perceptually takes place when there is an interaction between a presenter and perceiver is the context in which thoughts, feelings, verbal and nonverbal behaviors are experienced by each Self participating. This then is the appropriate context for us to study (together) the psych-phenomenon of **Defensiveness** – So . . . Let's get at it!

The foremost contention of Fr, PAT regarding DMs is that they all reside in our unconsciousness. In **my** way of thinking only the DM of **Repression** do I concede to the level of unconsciousness.

I think of Repression as it applies to **Repressed Memories (RM)** or **Repressed Impulses (RI)**. In the case of repressed memories, Posttraumatic Stress Disorder (PTSD) comes to mind – Where the individual is so traumatized by what happens to them that nothing of the event is knowingly processed by them. Essentially, it amounts to a happening that didn't happen (as far as they are concerned). I'm comfortable conceptualizing repression occurring in this fashion – The severity of the traumatic event mitigated by the DMs takes the mind and emotions down to a level of numbing unconsciousness.

Where repressed impulses are concerned, my mind sees a fundamental difference between these, which, conceptually, begin from the **inside out** and repressed memories, which begin from the **outside in**.

However, once memories and impulses are repressed within one's unconsciousness, the adaptive nature of the DMs is to keep them from surfacing, in either case.

The circular rationale of Fr and PAT for the existence of what, has been, or is repressed is – When, or if, it surfaces to a level above unconsciousness, it will bear witness to itself. We know it was **There** because it's now, **Here** – The inevitable byproduct of an airtight circular theory.

Denial is the only other DM that I am willing to concede an element that resembles unconsciousness. From the way I phrased this you can see I'm hedging on this one. Fr and PAT might say I'm **in denial** about this one. But to validate the way I'm leaning is to validate my awareness of the way I'm leaning – Toward awareness on some level above unconsciousness.

I might as well just come out and say this. It's hard for me to conceptualize denial occurring without some mitigator like **Suppression** (which I sometimes have referred to as conscious repression) – pushing it down to a lower level of awareness above unconsciousness.

I think I'm saying (without saying) that I'm more comfortable with putting denial with the other DMs that I believe do not reach the level of unconsciousness, but rather reside somewhere between unconsciousness and the outstretched fingertips of awareness.

DMs are not innate – But are acquired. They develop along with the rest of our personality. Our personality develops through person perception and self-experience.

Our personality is that which distinguishes us as a person. No two personalities are alike. Our personality may be dynamically described based upon the needs that emanate from it. These needs are acquired by a person based on their perception of what others perceive them to need.

Early on, the child perceives what their parent needs them to need. If the parent needs the child to do well – The child perceives the need to do well to be an important addition to the picture they're painting of themselves. Likewise with other needs the child perceives the parent needs the child to need: Like the need to please. The need to do and say the right thing. The need to succeed. The need to not fail. The need to try. The need to not quit, et al.

Needing-to-need-the-needs-the-**child**-perceives-the-**parent**-needs-them-to need – This perception is further driven home by continuous reinforcement to acquire them. Intermittent reinforcement keeps them going and growing – Imposing pressure on the child – First **Other**-imposed – Then **Self**-imposed.

Pressure: In the form of expectations, unrealistic and unmeasured, at times – Often untempered with sensitivity – Relentlessly unforgiving of any stumbles or shortfalls – Creates an atmosphere of anxiety and uncertainty about the status and security of Self in the scheme of things.

There's almost a certainty that if one's perception of one's Self is assailed and splattered by the brush of their perception of the other's perception of them – Their picture of themselves will be considerably diminished in quality and substance – A poor self-concept will result – And self-esteem will tumble.

The dual duty of our defenses is to protect our self-concept and alleviate our anxiety. To say this is accomplished on an unconscious level is to explain nothing. [To say that we may not be aware that, and how, our defenses are working is not the same as saying they're working on an unconscious level.]

In my mind, our defenses develop along with the rest of our personality through person perception and self-experience. **Defensiveness** to me is a way of **perceiving** and **interpreting** what we're perceiving. It mitigates perceptual fallout that might otherwise, if not reframed, do psychological damage to our psyche, self-concept, and self-worth. [Or so we think and are anxious that it might.]

The question arises – Do our defenses allow us to get the "**true picture**" of ourselves as we perceive others, our perception of their perception of us, and our perception of ourselves. Or, is **perceptual distortion** of some sort, inherent in **defensive perceiving** and **self-experiencing?**

Perceptual dissonance triggers **Defensiveness**. Dissonance intimates disharmony, discord, discrepancy amongst perceptions . . . Specifically I'm referencing perceptions we have of others' perceptions of us and perceptions we have of ourselves.

Keep in mind, early in our personality's development, through person perception and self-experience – In forming (painting) the picture of our Self – We relied heavily upon the paints our parents provided us with – when they presented to us the perceptions they had of us.

Our self-portrait, then, is a compilation of the needs our parents needed us to have. Subsequent to our acquiring these parent-favored needs, our parents intermittently presented us with the perceptual message that they needed us to grow these needs. If we did, we would be rewarded by their positive responses. We did, And we were (in most instances).

The perceptual dissonance arises when our perception of their perception of our presentation is that it does not measure up, and, therefore, our self-concept (our picture of ourselves) does not measure up to the one they primarily helped us paint.

Not measuring up means that in some way(s) we've come up short. An example at this point will make this ever so clear. Say one of our most important needs was **to please** our parents with what we said or did. On this occasion, we came up short. It was perceptually clear to us that our words and actions were not pleasing to them – But quite the opposite – They presented in their responses their disappointment and displeasure and perceptually conveyed this to us in no uncertain terms. We got their message, loud and clear – Resounding (as it were). Then clashing with their need – (which became our need) – To please and see ourselves as pleasing.

Switching metaphors – Look at what happens this way – Our self-portrait has been altered and looks different than it did before. We don't feel good about the "New look" or the Change we see in ourselves.

But, hold on, the scenario I have given lacks one important addition – **Defensiveness** has yet to play its role. [But if we let **Defensiveness** enter the picture we'll have to go back to the start and rewrite the script.]

Enter **Defensiveness** with its special way of perceiving things. The perception we initially said was perceptually clear – **Defensiveness** can make instantly hazy. Paradoxically, it filters out some of the clear – Deliberately making us less sure of what we're perceiving.

Being less sure of what we're perceiving from the one perceiving us leaves the door open for us to perceptually alter what we're perceiving. Altering our perception of the other's perception of us to the end that the way we need to see ourselves (to continue to feel good about ourselves) is preserved and protected. This is what **Defensiveness** is all about.

Once again understand that the way we need to see ourselves was instigated and subsequently reinforced by person perception and self-experience. Our self-concept was formed and grew from our perceptions of significant others' perceptions of us – Which for all intents and purposes became our perceptions of ourselves.

Whether our self-concept is a true and real picture of who we are, of course, is subject to validation. Our self-concept could very well be a compilation of both the **Real** and the **Ideal**. If there is more of the Ideal than the Real in our picture of our Self, there is more for us to live up to.

The Ideal Self is primarily the product of our perceptions of what significant others presented to us that we should be like. Starting with our parents, or parental substitutes – We were presented with shoulds and oughts. With do's and don'ts. With demands and projected expectations. All, intended to create a self-concept of which they and we, could be proud. That is, if we were able to meet their needs for us to need and think and feel and act, accordingly.

As long as parent and child are in sync about what the parent needs the child to need. And the child is pursuing that need in the way and to the extent the parent needs them to – the Ideal Self part of the self-concept is rewarded and becomes increasingly more important to the parent looking for it in the child's presentation (and to the child looking for it within themselves). The parent looks for the child to present the need to please. The parent is pleased when the child presents it. The child is pleased when the parent presents that they are pleased, and ends up being pleased with themselves. The Ideal Self of their self-concept has been satisfied and strengthened. The ante for presenting pleasing has been "upped."

Perceptual dissonance occurs when there's an alteration of perceptions – presented by the presenter or the perceiver. The perceiver's reaction becomes their presentation back to the presenter. The unanticipated, unexpected alteration of perception creates a different contingency of presentation and response in a given situation: The one expected to please – And be perceived as pleasing – And perceive the other as perceiving them pleasing – In reality has done, or said, something not pleasing – An alteration of perceptions occurs as well as perceptual dissonance. [When perceptual dissonance occurs can cognitive and emotional dissonance be far behind?]

Cognitive dissonance – When thoughts we had about ourselves clash with thoughts we're having about ourselves as we're experiencing perceptual dissonance.

Emotional dissonance – Feelings we had toward ourselves clash with feelings we're having about ourselves as we're experiencing perceptual dissonance.

If our commitment to perpetuate our Ideal-Self-part of our self-concept is resolute, and (we'd like to think) unflinching – Even a slight alteration of perceptions in a given situation can be unsettling – More than unsettling – Can be anxiety-producing.

How come this is so? Because when our picture of ourselves changes for the worse – So do our feelings about that picture. Our self-concept stumbles. And our self-worth tumbles. By now, I'm sure, you've got the picture of the Picture! On to more about how **Defensiveness** mitigates Dissonance.

My Wife's Behavior As A Child.
An Example Of Projection.

We are not born defensive. Nor is **Defensiveness** bred in our unconsciousness. It does occur and manifest itself very early in life. With my wife's permission in hand, I'd like to use a happening my wife shared with me that makes this point better than if I made it up. She related to me that she was just a toddler when (her mother was her witness) she put her first sentence together (subject with predicate).

Apparently something had gotten broken. Mother had discovered it and got upset. Her face, her gestures, the tone she used to express herself – "All right, who did it"? – All combined in one presentation – An angry person comin' at cha.

Present and accounted for, for this inquisition was my "toddler wife," her five-year-old brother, and mother, of course. The story goes, mother was particularly zeroed in on my wife. Mother swears that without hesitation, my "toddler wife" blurted the words – as she pointed to her brother – "Glen did it!" – Of course if the truth be told – My wife, Barbara, was the guilty party. Glen (this time anyway) had nothing to do with it.

Barb's mother had memorialized the event with an entry into her baby diary – Barb's words and picture included. There was Barbara – spanking clean in her frilly white dress – pointing her finger in her brother's direction – who stood there in his suspenders and overalls.

Could there be better evidence that **Defensiveness** is learned behavior! Unconscious? Baloney! The way I figure, Barbara as a toddler had seen and heard the sights and sounds of this scenario probably plenty of times before – With the players being mother getting after Glen for doing something wrong and Barb being spectator to the whole event – Mom pointing at Glen – Angrily asking him why he did it.

This time mother was pointing at her and looked and sounded angry. What's wrong with this picture! In Barb's mind was the other picture – The one she knew so well. So, in effect, by pointing her finger at Glen, and saying "Glen did it," she was reframing the picture as she remembered it from before.

Instead of talking about defense mechanisms, I talk about **Defensiveness** as a technique we develop over time. The technique when applied has a number of variations . . .

Defensiveness Ala Projection

The textbook term for the defensive technique Barbara used is **Projection**. This is a defensive technique that involves a person "throwing away" from themselves responsibility or blame that has been directed at them and diverting it towards someone or something else. It's like the shot directed at them ricochets off them and (with their guidance) ends up getting someone or something else, instead.

Whether this defensive technique is effective or not in transferring responsibility or blame depends on how well the presenter sells it and whether the perceiver is buying it. It does this much, however, even if the perceiver is not completely sold. It buys the presenter time to extricate themselves, temporarily at least, from the hot seat – Which relieves some of the anxiety – and keeps the self-concept and self-worth intact for the time being.

This underscores a facet of **Defensiveness** – That it brings only temporary relief. However, if this defense "works" for us time and again ("works," according to our perception) – Like other repetitive behaviors, this defensive technique becomes habitual – Which then in its presentation could be perceived as automatic and reflexive, like we were using it "unconsciously." Oh, we are aware all right. Well practiced. Got it down cold. Seeming like we could do it in our sleep.

To sum things up so far . . . We've established that **Defensiveness** arises when we experience perceptual dissonance – When our perception of the other's perception of us doesn't correspond with the perception we need to have of ourselves coming into the situation. **Defensiveness** arises to enable us to hang on to the picture we need to have of ourselves. This is important to us lest our perception of the other's perception of us alter that picture in some undesirable way.

Our defenses are there to keep the picture of ourselves – When we look at ourselves – Just the way we like it. Especially if our Ideal Self (the one our parents needed us to need) takes up most of the picture. **Defensiveness** does whatever it takes to perpetuate that picture from early childhood on.

I said there were variations of defensive techniques that rise to our defense, when our Self experiences perceptual dissonance – Which then spawns cognitive (thinking) and emotional (feeling) dissonance. We've only touched on one so far. Using my wife's "Glen did it" example I introduced to you the defensive technique called projection. I have a few more things to say about projection and then we'll move on to examining other defensive techniques commonly used to stave off anxiety and preserve the current picture of oneself. Let me underscore at this point that it is important to me – that it be important to you – To look very closely at these defensive techniques and see which ones you can relate to. [Don't let your **Defensiveness** deter you from doing this. It is important that we get to **Know Our Defenses**.]

Knowing Our Defenses

Back to Projection as a defensive technique. Check this. Check yourselves out on this one to see if it belongs in your defensive repertoire. The context in which this variation of **Defensiveness** is likely to occur is when – if we were to take ownership for what we've said or done – it would put us in a bad light to the one perceiving us (and to ourselves were we not to defend ourselves by not taking ownership). Thus, for example, if we overreact and lose our temper – And become very angry at the other for what they may have said or done – We may very well take it out on them – By shouting and making menacing gestures . . . You make me so angry! Why do you do this when you know it makes me angry! What's wrong with you! Do you want me to explode!

What's wrong with this picture? Doesn't the angry one have a right to be angry? The other one is probably getting what they deserve. Maybe it's hard to see what I want us to see because we've been there. Done that. Maybe we've been on both ends of something like this. I dare say in a situation like this both sides would be relying on their defenses.

The angry one is defensively hedging on taking ownership for the kind and degree of intensity of their reaction . . . **"You make me so angry."**

"You make me so angry." Speaking undefensively – No one can make us angry. It's hard for our defenses to let us see this – But we have a mediating ego which allows us to choose whether to become angry or not. Therefore, if we become angry in this particular situation – The Other may have been a precipitator – But we chose to get angry!

The intensity of our anger is the other aspect of our reaction – That undefensively, we need to take ownership for. If we're so angry that we're ready to explode, we are responsible for letting ourselves get to this point.

I sense that some of us are not liking nor agreeing with what I'm saying. Could it be – Our **Defensiveness** at work! [Projection is doing its job even as I write, and you read what I write]

The one on the other end of our "angry" probably is using the same defense we are – Projecting away from themselves some of the anger directed at them – thus blunting its impact some (As all "good defenses" do).

There's another way that projection is used that you might not have thought about before. It happens when we project upon the Other – attributes that may be physical, mental, emotional, social, moral – That we want – That we need them to have. That (Here's where **Defensiveness** comes in) they may not have – It's like seeing what we need to see. Whereas if we were to see the Other as they really are, we would experience perceptual dissonance.

Why does "love is blind" come into my mind right about now! You can see how this particular brand of **Defensiveness** is potentially problematic for both parties in the relationship. Neither, in this scenario, really knows what they're getting in the other, if they're into the practice of projecting.

Defensiveness Ala Displacement

Ever had a rough day at work where whoever's over you used their position of power to dress you down, and mercilessly rake you over the coals, for either something that wasn't your fault – Or if it was – from your perspective it wasn't that big a deal. It certainly didn't merit the magnitude of their reaction.

You weren't given the opportunity to respond. You had to just stand there and take it. How did it feel? It felt s____. That's how it felt. You felt degraded. Frustrated. Powerless. And very angry.

You came home that night still steaming from the buildup of your suppressed anger. From the moment you stepped through the door, you acted like a caged tiger, lashing out at whoever came by – Your Other – Your children. It didn't matter – They all were fair game! [You, my friend, were displaying the defensive technique of **Displacement**.]

You had to hold it in, at your job. It was tough on you. But you did it. You wanted to let them have it. But that would have been disastrous. So you brought your thoughts and feelings home with you and took your frustration and anger out on a "safer" target. They got it – just because they were around to get it. Defensively, as soon as they figured out what was happening, they cut you a wide berth, and left you alone, (temporarily – to stew) – (That is, if they knew what was good for them).

Later on, when we cool down, we realize how we took it out on those who had absolutely nothing to do with it. And we feel badly and hopefully apologize for our behavior. Not as an excuse, but as an explanation.

Defensiveness Ala "Sour Grapes" Rationalization

Once upon a time we had this relationship with an Other whom we perceived to have all the characteristics we desired in an Other. We probably put them on a pedestal and felt they could do no wrong. We thought they felt as strongly about us as we about them.

But they let us down. Unexpectedly. Unceremoniously. They dumped us. One moment we thought we had the real thing. The next moment we stood there empty-hearted.

How could this be! Our mind and heart struggled for answers, but there were none that made any sense. Anxiety, disappointment, hurt, sadness began to convert into resentment and anger. How could they have done this to us, after we had invested so much! What's wrong with them that they could do such a thing! We didn't deserve this. Maybe we really didn't know this person as well as we thought we did. Maybe they weren't "all that" to begin with!

This, my friend, is a prime example of another defensive technique at work to alleviate our anxiety and preserve our self-concept . . . **Sour Grapes Rationalization**.

The person who we once perceived could "walk on water" has taken a mighty plunge in our estimation. They had to sink so that we could continue swimming. The higher we once built them up – the further they have fallen – as we look at them in hindsight through our defensive eyes.

Defensiveness Ala Sweet Lemon Rationalization

It's happened before. It can happen again . . . That after a period of time, perchance, we meet up again. And whatever worked for us, at first, seems to be working again . . . [Once smitten; twice smitten.]

Now, would you listen to us! . . . We can't say enough good things about the Other – as we sing their praises. We've got a name for this too – We call this defensive technique **"Sweet Lemon" Rationalization**. Whatever dissonance we once experienced has been converted into "defensive lemonade."

Defensiveness Ala Reaction Formation

"The lady doth protest too much" – brings to mind still another defensive technique called **Reaction Formation**. This speaks of an incongruency between what one is thinking and feeling **inside** – and what one is saying and doing **outside**. The person who ostensibly says, "I don't care," is defensively covering up for the fact and feeling that they do care. They may be afraid to show that side of themselves – Thinking and feeling that were they to do it – It would make them vulnerable.

Specifically, "The lady doth protest too much" refers to an aspect of this defensive technique that is typified by one who outwardly in words and actions goes "overboard" in their protestations in a defensive attempt to cover up, and compensate for, unacceptable thoughts, desires and impulses that may lurk inside. They stand on a "soap box" outside, to soap and cleanse themselves inside.

Defensiveness Ala Sublimation

There is a defensive technique that is uniquely different from the others in that it succeeds (relatively speaking) in perceptually redirecting undesirable impulses. That would be **sublimation**.

We who have aggressive, competitive personalities are able through this defensive technique to channel these needs into socially acceptable outlets. Contact sports would be an example. [The caveat would be that one would still be in control of oneself in this context.]

Defensiveness Ala Undoing

It's not my problem; I had nothing to do with it. Besides, even if there were a remote chance that I was minimally involved in what happened; there's nothing I can do about it now; I can't undo what has been done.

Some of us defensively try to **undo** the unacceptable act or the potential harm inherent in thinking about the unacceptable act – by doing good. In effect trying to make up for – to replace as it were – to undo that which was bad. This defensive technique is appropriately called **undoing.**

Defensiveness Ala Lying

I'd like to include in our list of defensive techniques – **lying**. Have you had the experience of having all the circumstantial evidence you need to draw only one conclusion – and confronted the person with it – only to have them lie to your face?

Some have reported – parents with children – actually catching their child in the act only to have them lie about having anything to do with it. Either we have a child having an out-of-touch-with-reality-experience, or we have a habituated, automatic reflexive defensive technique that flies in the face of reality.

Summing Up So Far What We Have Learned About Our Defenses As We Get To Know Them

If our intent is **Knowing Our Defenses** then let's review what we have learned so far about the various defensive techniques. In general the purpose of a defensive technique is to distort perceptual reality – In so doing – Reduce the amount of perceptual dissonance experienced, along with the cognitive and emotional dissonance that come with it.

How our **Defensiveness Works Ala Our Defenses** – (e.g. Projection). It reduces perceptual dissonance because its user can defensively pretend the presenter had someone or something else in mind than the user – when blaming or assigning responsibility. [This is essentially what the user is doing – when they project blame and responsibility for the outcome on someone or something else]. Reflect on this defensive technique to see if it fits you, or your Other.

Displacement involves taking the frustration, anxiety, and anger that your perception of the other's perception of you elicited in you and transferring it onto the other – who had no involvement with what happened to you – But now, because they have the misfortune to be in your presence are experiencing the second-hand fallout. How come they are your choice? Because they're a much safer target upon which to vent. Because they're there, when you're feeling the way you do.

Sour Grapes and Sweet Lemon Rationalizations refer to the off again, on again, cold and hot, flip flop nature of the change in our thinking. Our tendency to alter our thinking about the Other is born out of our need to defend the change in our perceptions . . . of the Other; the perceptions of the Other of us; our perceptions of ourselves. We must justify our vacillating thoughts and feelings by coming up with plausible reasons for the change.

When we overreact to something said or done that strikes a chord within us, our **Defensiveness** tends to give us away (as it were). It reveals in our reactive presentation strong thoughts and feelings that reside within. The form of our reaction gives this variation of **Defensiveness** its name – **Reaction Formation**.

The defensive technique of **Sublimation** is perhaps the easiest understood, and of the defensive techniques the one that (if we're using) – we get the least defensive about. The key to this is that we're channeling our otherwise marginally acceptable behaviors and impulses into societally acceptable activities.

Lying outright, reiterating half-truths in a defensive desire to alleviate our anxiety and preserve our self-concept involves ultimately lying to ourselves, keeping us from perceiving the truth about ourselves.

There's one more defensive technique that I have yet to mention – and that would be – **To take our Defense on the Offense**. This is characterized by attacking back when we perceive the other attacking us. If you have tried this defensive technique, I'm sure you would agree – Of all, it is the least effective.

How come it's least effective? Because our defensive techniques are primarily used in the hope that we'll look better to the Other and to ourselves. When we attack we may be temporarily putting the

Other back on their heels, but we surely don't look better to them nor to ourselves.

As Far As You're Concerned

If one or another of these defensive techniques jumps out at you – That you can identify with, and say – That's mine – That's what I do to defend myself – Then you're well on the way to knowing your defenses. If you have trouble relating to any of them – Why not ask your Other, what they have noticed about you, along the way – that has been defensive in nature. You do the same for your Other – That's how we get to **Know Our Defenses**.

Knowing Our Defenses, contrary to what we may have thought, doesn't really help us know ourselves better. Remember, the job of **Defensiveness** is to distort our perceptions. I hope I'm not confusing you too badly – But here it goes anyway. Our defenses arise to distort our perception – Which before our defenses came to our rescue was causing perceptual dissonance. That's the way this works. When we initially perceive the other perceiving us in a manner that runs counter to the way we need to see ourselves and feel about ourselves, we experience perceptual dissonance (which includes cognitive and emotional dissonance as well).

That's the way it would be and stay that way were it not for our defenses – whose job it is to reduce our perceptual dissonance. How? By distorting our perceptions. Some choice, eh? Perceptual dissonance or perceptual distortion. Or, is there another alternative that would help us modify (even if we can't completely resolve) our perceptual dilemma? That's what we'll be exploring next as we consider the efficacy of **Lowering Our Defenses**.

Lowering Our Defenses

Once we know our defenses then we can lower our defenses. Question is why would we want to? Don't our defenses serve a vital purpose in our lives, i.e. to alleviate anxiety and protect and preserve our self-concept? Sounds important enough to me – I'm sure, to you, too.

The problem is that unless and until we lower our defenses, we won't be able to get a **true** picture of ourselves – Nor a **true** picture of how others see us. Remember how we've said that our defenses distort our perception of how others perceive us and distort our perception of how we see ourselves. They distort our perceptions to reduce the perceptual dissonance (cognitive and emotional) we experience when our perceptions of how others perceive us clash with the perceptions we need to have of ourselves when we are perceived or we perceive – [Which for the most part represent the Ideal-Self portion of our self-concept.]

Putting this more succinctly . . .If we were to have our defenses taken away from us, the perceptual dissonance we would experience could very well be more than we can bear. Because of this, I'm not advocating – Let's get rid of our defenses! I can't imagine that we could, even if we wanted to. I am saying that we need to lower them, however, in order to reduce the distortion. Reducing the distortion, however, means that perceptual dissonance can have at us unhampered by defense – Which means that we'll have to find another way to handle it.

If perceptual dissonance increases as we lower our defense – What does this avail us? It gives us a truer, more objective, realistic perception of ourselves (as we see others see us and as we see ourselves). Ironic, isn't it – that in lowering our defenses we are daring ourselves to see the perceptions we were going to such lengths to protect ourselves from seeing!

That's the essence of the trade-off . . . Lowering our defense means that we will be opening ourselves up to more perceptual dissonance. However, without adulteration by our defenses (at least not as much as before) we'll be getting a truer perception of the other's perceptions of us and our perceptions of ourselves – Which is an important step forward toward our ultimate goal of being able to trust our perceptions.

Bottom line is, we can't trust perceptions that are heavily distorted – Not even moderately distorted. We'll probably have to settle for mildly distorted. Because having no defenses, at all, is not a viable option.

Keep in mind that our goal is to be able to trust our perceptions to the end that we may see ourselves as we really are. We're talking **Real Self** here. Not **Ideal Self**.

How we became the way we are, I covered in my second book (Seeing Ourselves As We See Others See Us). In case you're one of the "few" that hasn't read it yet ☺, I'll briefly review: Our self-concept from early in life, and on, is primarily comprised of perceptions we had of how parents or parent substitutes, perceived us. I.e. We perceived ourselves and subsequently presented ourselves as we perceived they needed to see us and needed us to see ourselves.

This is the self-concept, comprised mostly of Ideal Self that we strove for and even now may continue to strive for up to the present time. Our defenses arose from our need to be perceived by others and perceive ourselves along these same lines.

Our Ideal Self we know. Our Real Self is a whole other story. Few of us know our Real Self that well. Some don't know their Real Self at all. All of us could benefit from knowing our Real Self better. [We get to know our Real Self better by lowering our defenses and trusting our perceptions.]

Time for an example . . . Suppose we are one who early on in our personality development acquired a large need to please. Our parents needed to see us this way. Consequently, we needed to see ourselves this way. The need to please, therefore, became an integral part of our self-concept – i.e. of the way we needed to be perceived by others, and perceive ourselves . . . the Pleaser!

Now then, let's fast forward to a situation in which we are interacting with a significant other (in this case, significant in the sense that how they perceive us is very important to us.) Continuing our example . . . We need this person to perceive us as a pleasing person. However, something we must have either said or done – From their perspective has not pleased them. [An interaction is a function of what each person brings to the situation. In this case, we are bringing our need to please. The other is bringing their need to let us know that we have not pleased them.]

We are caught off guard – We had no idea, coming in, that this would be the nature of the other's presentation. Our perception of the other's perception of us is that we're displeasing. This strikes at the core of how we need to perceive ourselves. Perceptual dissonance occurs – The way we perceive the other perceiving us is not the way we need to perceive ourselves.

Our defenses arise to come to our rescue. We may offer excuses for why we said or did it. We may blame our behavior on the circumstances, or on someone else. We may deny it altogether – Distorting perceptions to reduce perceptual dissonance, alleviate anxiety, preserve our self-concept.

I'm giving myself license to rewrite this real life script just a bit. Lowering our defenses would enable us to perceive the perception of us – the other is presenting – as being a true and real perception of us based upon how they perceived what we said or did. This is the **past** perception of us they are presently sharing with us.

Lowering our defenses and trusting our perceptions (so far so good) we are perceiving their past perception of us – that they're presenting us – as true and real to them – and, therefore, worthy of being compared with our perception of ourselves in this regard.

Lowering our defenses we can trust our perception of ourselves. In retrospect we can see how what we said or did was, in reality, displeasing. Looking at our self-concept, we can see the largeness of our need to please. And we can begin to understand what is at the heart of our perceptual dissonance.

We grow in understanding and accepting our Real Self when we are able to lower our defenses and trust our perception. The self-concept we need to see – and need others to see in us – so much so, that our defenses become an integral habitual part of our everyday presentation – By lowering our defenses and trusting our perceptions there is less perceptual dissonance from the start. It's less important that we perceive ourselves a Pleaser. It becomes less important that others perceive us this way. Therefore, when we perceive they don't, we don't have to become defensive. Our modified self-concept – more Real than Ideal – now, presents us with a picture of ourselves as having less of a need to please. Realistically accepting that there have been – are – will be – times when what we say or do is anything but pleasing.

Let's say that your favorite defense has been (may still be) **Projection**. This would mean that when you're put on the spot (or the proverbial hot seat) by someone, whose perception of you matters to you – You tend to heat up with anxiety. And then hoping your body language doesn't give you away, quick thinking (albeit defensive thinking) saves your day – as you find something or someone else to shift responsibility to – or blame.

Lowering your defenses will allow you to: Gather yourself, inside yourself. Listen to what the Other has to say. Find your assertiveness center. And come forward with a willingness to take on the responsibility that is yours. And if that is not enough to satisfy and the Other is willing to explore other options for assigning the responsibilities that were not yours – So much the better.

From my perspective, defensive techniques, over-employed, habituate to such an extent that they become second nature to us. Because they are best at delivering quick, temporary relief from anxiety – and short-term protection of the picture we need to have of ourselves – we are understandably reluctant to even lower them – let alone, give them up.

Hey, nobody's said anything about having to give them up. Even if you could – But you can't – I don't want you to. Just lower them, my reader. That's all I want you to do. Those of you who like to do things in a big way – Don't even try to do more than you can. Believe me, lowering them is enough of a challenge.

Lower them and then learn how to **Live with Them**.

Remember that when you lower your defenses, you can then begin to trust your perceptions. When your defenses are higher, they distort your perceptions in order to reduce perceptual dissonance. In effect defenses then perpetuate an unrealistic, idealistic perception of ourselves – i.e. our Ideal Self takes over our self-concept – leaving us little room for our Real Self to be shown. Our defenses see to that.

It's a very different story and a very different picture of ourselves that arises when we lower our defenses. Absent the anxious need we have had to perpetuate that Ideal picture of ourselves (that we believe we needed others to perceive in us) – We begin to question whether it has been more the **Other's** need to see us in a particular light – than our **own** need to see ourselves in that light – That has led us to call upon our defenses to perpetuate a picture of ourselves – That wasn't the Real deal.

Here's a synopsis of how this whole thing plays out. To really know ourselves – i.e. to get the true and real picture of ourselves – we must lower our defenses. To lower our defenses we need to know which ones we employ. Once they're lowered, we can begin to trust our perceptions. When we are able to trust our perceptions then we can know who we **really are**.

Knowing Our Defenses. Lowering Our Defenses. Living With Our Defenses. A three-step program for getting to know our **True Selves**. "True" in the sense that our self-concept portrays a picture of ourselves that has demonstrably narrowed the gap between our Ideal and Real Selves – Therefore depicting a Self representing who we really are. This then would be a picture of ourselves that we would not have to protect against others seeing . . . What you see, is who I am – Is what you get!

When I'm busy defending myself, you don't get to see the **Real Me**. I don't get to see the Real Me. That's because it's not the Real Me that I'm defending. It's the Me I think you need Me to be; It's the Me I think I need Me to be.

I don't put the Real Me out there when I perceive you want to see the **Other Me** – The Me I perceive you need Me to be. The Me I think I should therefore be – The **Ideal Me** I get defensive about when I see you see something else in Me.

In my book Don't Be A Stranger (To Yourself) I write about the steps we need to take to get to know ourselves: Go outside ourselves – to get inside ourselves – and then turn ourselves inside out – Getting to know ourselves through person perception and self-experience. Remember, when we lower our defenses we can trust our perceptions – our perceptions of others' perceptions of us – our perceptions of others – our perceptions of ourselves.

"What you see is what you get" can be the mantra of a well-adjusted psychologically healthy individual – Provided it's not put out there in an in-your-face-sort-of-way. This would be the case, if the individual is implying: I am who I am. I'm not going to change. You're certainly not going to get me to change. Accept me, or forget it. [Taken in this way – "What you see is what you get" could be perceived as a defensive ploy to have the person, perceiving, look no further inside the presenter.]

Contrariwise – "What you see is what you get" can mean that the person perceives themselves as not hiding anything – feeling good about the fact that they have nothing to hide.

This is good that we present as we perceive ourselves to be. If we know ourselves, having lowered our defenses, to be a **caring** person, then this is the way we should present ourselves! The person who says they don't care – when, inside themselves, they really do care – is being defensive – perhaps protecting their own vulnerability.

Some personality characteristics are much easier to present than others. Another way of expressing this is to say that when we look at the picture of ourselves – some portions are softer on our eyes than others. **Kind** is something we like to see each time we look. **Quick to anger** is something part of us wishes our defenses wouldn't let us see. All we can hope to say is – We're working on it.

Those of us who have this thing about not making any mistakes – Take a lowered defensive look at ourselves and see . . . Mistakes – We've made quite a few. What a load off our shoulders – That we've been able to cut down on our excuses. And when we make the inevitable next mistake – Admit it to others and to ourselves – And try not to make the same mistake again – If we can help it.

Avoidance – Mother Of All Defenses

One of the most common of defenses – That I can't believe I forgot to mention. But I did. And by talking about it now, instead of letting it go (and you might not have been the wiser for it) – I'm going to lower my defenses and bring it to your attention, albeit belatedly.

Would you believe the coincidence that the defensive technique I'm about to talk about is **Avoidance**. Avoidance – the Mother of all defenses. It's the defense that has a direct connection to all the other defenses – But takes what the others are designed to do one step further. The others are there to alleviate the anxiety precipitated by their **participation** in the event – The anxiety occurs in **experiencing** the event – The **Defensiveness** arises to alleviate **Participant Anxiety**.

The defense of Avoidance allows us to avoid participant anxiety altogether. It doesn't, however, help us as much where **Anticipatory Anxiety** is involved – Which is spawned by the anxiety we have when we allow ourselves even to think about becoming a participant. At this point we need extra defensive help from one or more of our other defenses.

An example will make this "clearer than mud." [I don't mean this literally.] Suppose we're one who gets very anxious at social gatherings when we know hardly any people there. If we anticipate this might be the case with an up-coming event – We might say – We're not going. Our excuse (rationalizing) is that it sounds boring. There won't be anyone to talk to, etc. We're defending ourselves from getting anxious by avoiding the event altogether. We're trying to alleviate anticipatory anxiety by making excusive statements to ourselves.

[Makes sense – It's all pretty straightforward – Avoid participant anxiety by avoiding becoming a participant.] If this is social anxiety that we're talking about avoiding, we can see how **Defensive Avoidance** may be adaptive in the short-term, but maladaptive in the long run. The nature of this particular defense is that – if taken to the extreme [in colloquial terms] – We end up living an extremely sheltered if not solitary life. In this instance

Defensiveness is keeping **anxiety – out – But ourselves – in**.

Let me expand on the trade-off exemplified in defenses being adaptive in the short-term, maladaptive in the long run. It's extremely important that we understand the implication of this distinction, especially since, like it or not, we'll be living with our defenses.

Living With Our Defenses

Living with our defenses does not equate with **living defensively**. If our defenses remain high, we will be sacrificing too much of living at the altar of anxiety. We will be paying homage to the preservation of our Self while dishonoring the growth and expansion of our Self.

Our defenses, understand, protect a self-concept which if we could look at it, less defensively (trusting our perceptions) – We might see things about ourselves that we might want to change. Or, we might see ourselves differently than we saw others see us – [Now that we have lowered our defenses and are trusting our perceptions.]

Does this make sense? I think it does. Looking at ourselves defensively is like looking at something we're afraid to look at. When we lower our defenses, and trust our perceptions, we get a much clearer picture of who we are, of what we're like. It's clearer and more realistic, to boot, because we haven't had to distort it – first – With our defenses.

Seeing ourselves as we see others see us – When we lower our defenses and trust our perceptions – May not match up that well with the way we now see ourselves. Others may still see us as **they** have needed (more than we) to see us. They bring their need to perceive us in a certain light (which no longer shines on us, at least not as brightly). So, they present, and we perceive, their disappointment.

Heretofore, defensively, trusting **their** perceptions, we would have been quick to add **our** disappointment in us, to **theirs**. Lowering our defenses, trusting our perceptions, we begin to see their disappointment in us fits the picture **they** need to have of us, but not **as much** (we're working toward, **no longer**) the picture we have of ourselves. They have been projecting on us the picture they need to have of us. Defensively, we took it on because we needed very much for them to see us as they did – But in the process our perceptions of ourselves became distorted.

Lowering our defenses and trusting our perceptions we begin to see ourselves as we really are. Our perception may not be their perception of us but that's becoming increasingly OK with us. More and more we're liking what we see. The gap between our Ideal Self and Real Self has narrowed.

All along we have thought we needed our defenses to protect us from others and ourselves. Seeing ourselves as we really are – We are coming to realize that the perceptions of us that others present us with may be more a function of how others (with their specific personality needs) need to perceive us than they are a representation of how we really are.

Maybe we'd be better off if we stopped looking at ourselves though **other's** eyes. Here's a novel idea. How about looking at ourselves with our **own** eyes. That's precisely what we're doing when we lower our defenses and trust our perceptions.

Living with our defenses versus **living defensively** depicts two significantly different perspectives – On how we intend to live our lives. In the case of **living with our defenses** this implies that we take ownership for our choices. That for the most part we stay in charge of ourselves – That in general, when we look at ourselves with lowered defenses we like what we see. Of course there's always room for improvement. We view our life as a process. Our goal is to keep on growing – Accepting the reality that as long as we live and breathe we are a work in progress. We still feel the need to bring our defenses along for the ride! We accept the fact that as human beings we are neither brave enough – Nor foolish enough – to try to go on without them.

But we view none of this to be the same as living defensively. **Living defensively** would strongly suggest that we had made no progress in getting on top of our defenses – So they can't run away with us. When they pop up – (as they surely still will) – We will recognize them for what they are. Catch ourselves in the act of being defensive. Before it takes us too far – Becomes second nature to us – Or becomes the way we live our lives.

Living with our defenses under our conscious control means that we can be more direct. More open. More honest. We can be more accountable. More responsible. More dependable. More trustworthy. All these good things to be. Not because we need first and foremost for others to see us this way. Not even because we need to see ourselves this way. But because **We in reality are becoming – to be – this way**. [Lowering our defenses, and trusting our perceptions, we present ourselves as we perceive ourselves to be.]

Are there things about ourselves that we would like to change, I certainly would hope so. It is not as though we already have arrived. Life is a process that is on-going. Our personalities one would hope are still expanding. We are not just getting older – We are growing older. We are like "the little train that could" – We keep on going and growing.

How many times already have you been told or you have told others – "You're just being defensive" – a living testimony to the reality that **Defensiveness** is a **fact** of life. So be it. But let's not let it **for us** become a **way** of life.

Blessings
Take Good Care,
Doc Ken
K. L. Fischer, PhD

About the Author

- Dr. Kenneth L. Fischer (affectionately called Doc Ken) has been in helping professions his entire adult life.

- Founder and pastor of Peace Lutheran Church, Disco, MI

- Pastor of Mt. Olive Lutheran Church, Grand Rapids, MI

- Junior High School teacher 8th grade English, 9th grade Latin, Muskego, MI

- First psychologist in the history of the Men's Unit, State Prison, Lowell, FL

- Dr. Fischer received his PhD in Personality Psychology, Michigan State University, East Lansing, MI

- His doctoral work was in Person Perception

- An instructor and lecturer, Dept. of Psychology, University of Wisconsin, Milwaukee, WI

- Also taught at various colleges throughout the Milwaukee-Metro area, namely Milwaukee Area Technical College, Mt. Mary College, Alverno College, and at Carthage College, Racine, WI

- Dr. Fischer has been a practicing psychologist in his own clinic for the past thirty-five years, treating adult couples and individuals

- ☐ His areas of expertise are in Personality and Person Perception

- ☐ His specialty is Personality Disorders

- ☐ Support Therapy Clinic is located in Hartland, WI

Other Books by Kenneth L. Fischer, PhD

Closeness Without Control:
The Key To A Loving Reciprocal Relationship Of
Assertive Independent Equals

Seeing Ourselves As We See Others See Us:
Our Personality Develops Through Person Perception
and Self-Experience

The Gray Area Of Psychological Abuse:
Abusee? Abuser? Or Both? How Can We Tell?
What Can We Do?

**Psychologically Speaking What Are We
Really Saying?**
The Music Behind The Music Behind Our Words

Don't Like The Way It Is - Change It:
Changing Before Or After An Ultimatum

We've Got Personality!
Now What?

Don't Be A Stranger (To Yourself):
Go Outside Yourself To Get Inside Yourself Then Turn
Yourself Inside Out

**The Art And Efficacy Of Managing Person
Perceptions:**
Manipulation In Its Highest Psychotherapeutic Sense

The Incomparable Spunkerface and Company:
Heaven Sent - Heaven Bent

Lamenting The Loss of Loyalty:
Where Has All The Loyalty Gone?!